This book belongs to:

Li*e HErb*t

Published by Ladybird Books Ltd
A Penguin Company
Penguin Books Ltd, 80 Strand, London WC2R 0RL, UK
Penguin Books Australia Ltd, Camberwell, Victoria, Australia
Penguin Books (NZ) Ltd, Cnr Airbourne and Rosedale Roads, Albany, Auckland, 1310, New Zealand

1 3 5 7 9 10 8 6 4 2

© LADYBIRD BOOKS MMIV

Printed in China

Amazing Plants

written by Lorraine Horsley
illustrated by Paul Cheshire

Ladybird

Here is a little seed in the ground.

6

The biggest
seed in the
world is the
Coco de mer.
It is as big as
a football.

The seed needs warmth
to help it grow.
A little root grows down
in the ground.

The roots of big trees stop the trees from falling over!

9

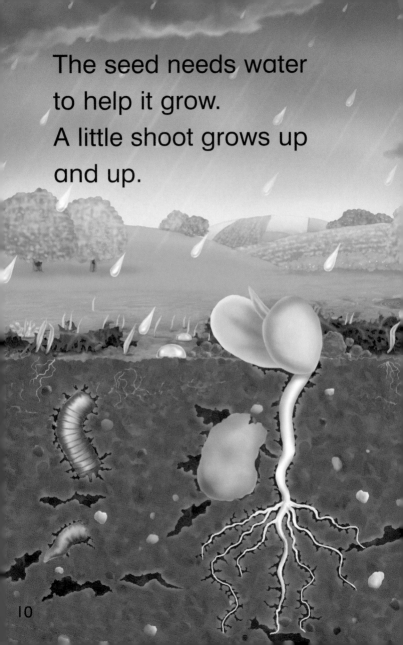

The seed needs water
to help it grow.
A little shoot grows up
and up.

10

Shoots always grow up even if the seed is planted upside down!

1

2

3

Here is the little plant with
two green leaves.
The little plant grows up
and up.

The fastest
growing plant
is Bamboo.
It can grow
one metre
a day!

The plant needs sunlight
to help it grow.
The sunlight helps the leaves
to make food.

The leaves of the Giant Waterlily
are as big as a paddling pool.

15

Here is a the plant with little flower buds. The plant grows up and up and the flower buds start to open.

The slowest flowering
plant in the world is
the Puya Raimondii.
It takes up to 150
years to flower!

Here is the plant with
little white flowers.

The biggest flower in
the world is the
Rafflesia.
It is as big as
a tractor wheel.

The little white flowers
make pollen.
Plants need pollen to make
new seeds.

Pollen grains are
so small that
hundreds of them
could sit on your
little finger tip.

21

Here is the plant. It is old and the flowers are starting to die.

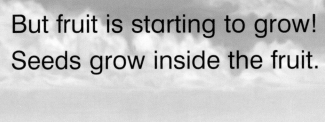

But fruit is starting to grow!
Seeds grow inside the fruit.

24

This fruit is a pod.

This seed is a bean.

25

The fruit dries up and
the seeds pop out.

The smallest seeds
in the world come
from an orchid.
They are as small
as specks of dust.

A little seed is in the ground.

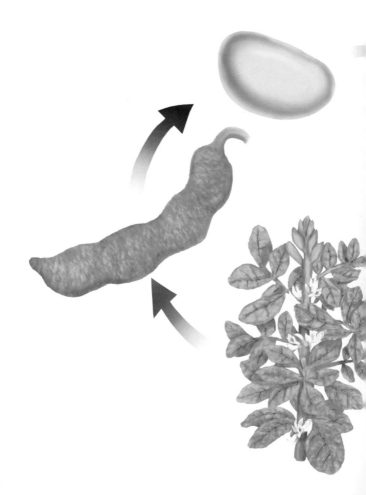

Do you know what
happens next?

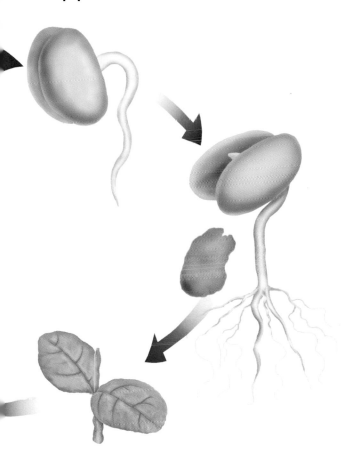

Glossary

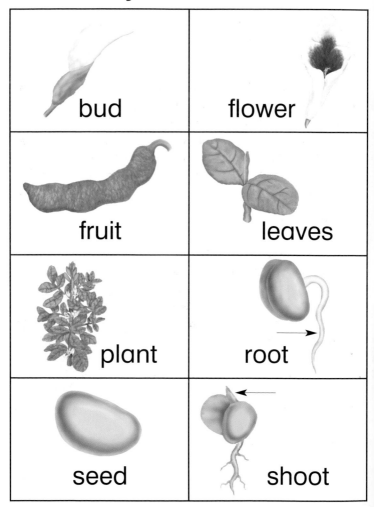

bud	flower
fruit	leaves
plant	root
seed	shoot